DIANA
REMEMBERED 1961–1997

The Daily Telegraph

DIANA

REMEMBERED 1961–1997

MACMILLAN

First published 1997 by Macmillan
an imprint of Macmillan Publishers Ltd
25 Eccleston Place, London SW1W 9NF
and Basingstoke

Associated companies throughout the world

ISBN 0 333 73474 2

A CIP catalogue record for this book is available from the British Library.

Designed by Derek Copsey, Omnific

CONTRIBUTORS

Sandra Barwick, Caroline Davies, Elizabeth Grice, Hilary Alexander and Colin Randall are all senior staff journalists on the *Daily Telegraph* and were part of the reporting team covering the events in the aftermath of the death of Diana, Princess of Wales.

W F Deedes has had a long association with the *Daily Telegraph* as writer, columnist and former editor, and was a personal friend of the Princess.

PICTURE ACKNOWLEDGEMENTS

The Publishers and the *Daily Telegraph* would like to thank the following:

Alpha for pictures on pages 51; AP for pictures on pages 108 (Johnny Eggitt), 110 (Neville Elder); Camera Press for pictures on pages 17, 30, 35 (Patrick Demarchelier), 38 & 40 (Snowdon), 42, 64, 66 (Snowdon); Cassidy & Leigh for pictures on pages 116 ; Anwar Hussein for pictures on pages 21, 26, 32, 33, 45, 56, 57;Ian Jones/*Daily Telegraph* for pictures on pages 9, 53, 58, 59, 60, 61, 63, 70, 75, 76, 77, 81, 82, 84, 89, 92, 93, 100, 106, 115, 117, 118, 119;Mirror Syndication International for pictures on pages 52, 55;National Portrait Gallery for pictures on page 120 (David Bailey);News Team International for pictures on page 112 (Steve Hill);Nunn Syndication for pictures on pages 55, 57;Press Association for pictures on pages 7,11, 12, 13, 14, 15, 16, 19, 22, 27, 28, 36, 39, 41, 44, 46, 69 (John Stillwell), 74 & 75(Martin Keene), 83 & 85 & 86 (John Stillwell), 95 (Tony Harris); Popperfoto for pictures on 23 (Snowdon), 25, 68 (Dylan Martinez), 87 (Damir Sagoli), 88 (Ian Waldie), 90 (John Pryke), 94;Reuters for pictures on pages 98 (Russell Boyce), 107; Rex Features for pictures on pages 20, 47, 48, 56, 78, 79; Star Images for pictures on page 94 (Ian Spark); Sygma for pictures on 65 (J L Atlan); *Sunday Telegraph*/Craig Stennett for picture on page 72; *The Daily Telegraph* 78 (Srdja Djukanovik), 97& 104 (Stephen Lock), 99 (Jim Winslett), 101 (Roy Letke), 102 (Chris Laurens), 103 (Brian Smith), 110 (Peter Orme), 111 (David Burgess); Universal Pictorial Press for pictures on pages 37

INTRODUCTION
W. F. Deedes

It was a life, when we think about it, of extraordinary contrasts. There were the troughs of despair. There were also peaks of delight. There were times when she appeared publicly to be inflicting wounds on herself. There were moments when she seemed sublime.

That is why the life of Diana, Princess of Wales, was such an *intriguing* life, to take a word from the Bidding Prayer at her funeral; and that is what makes this life worth close study. Notwithstanding all that has been written about her and the pictures taken in all her moods, there remained a faint aura of mystery about her. There were facets of her life we shall never fully comprehend.

It is false to her memory to pretend she was some sort of saint. She had a full share of human frailties – and the added misfortune, which most of us are spared, of having most of them paraded before an eager public eye.

Yet some of us who saw her at work came to admire the disciplines Diana imposed upon herself. She never overcame her fear of cameras, yet she trained herself to look at them as if she were enjoying it – trained herself so well, indeed, that photographers could blithely reassure themselves and others that she actually enjoyed the experience.

Her early life was clouded by the loss of her mother through divorce; a blow from which she never entirely recovered. Her young life was caught up first in the royal circle where she felt ill at ease; and then by a highly publicised broken marriage. Because she was by nature shy and haunted by a sense of her own inadequacies, this last experience caused her agony.

There followed the deepest trough of all when Diana seemed hardly to know what she was saying. There was a sort of desperate carelessness in the way she exposed her inner feelings to those whom she imagined to be on her side. Such petty victories as she won in that war of words were pyrrhic, every one of them. Out of this

darkness came a dawn. She transmuted her main weakness into a strength. Those who suffered, feared and trembled found they could communicate with someone who so well understood the feeling. She was a royal person, yet level with them.

I saw this side of her given full expression when, in the last month of her life, she went to Bosnia to talk with those injured or bereaved by landmines. Part of the gift was listening patiently, as so few of us ever do. Oh, the tales of woe and torment some of these victims of a bitter civil war were longing to impart.

It is a happy thought that during this last mission of her's there were unfolded the warmest of her gifts to humanity – the compassionate look, a touch of the hand, and the sort of warm embrace she gave the lonely sightless child afflicted with cerebral palsy whom we found lying on the makings of a bed in a Bosnian village. It was an embrace that came from the heart and communicated itself to the child. The cameras were far away.

There was a touch of stoicism there as well. Some of the tales we had to hear from victims of mines were so grisly that I turned my mind elsewhere. Diana's attention never flagged. Throughout the most painful recitals, she bore the look of a patient but kindly nurse.

She was able to offer this unique mixture of royalty – very important – with those of a young woman who never ceased to feel vulnerable. She came so close to all of us, yet had this way of soaring away, for which so many yearn. Precisely why we loved her is hard to define and not all that important. Pascal had one answer: "The heart has its reasons which reason knows nothing of."

Her final gift, we may think, was to inspire that funeral service in Westminster Abbey. There was a touch of genius in the arrangements for that closing hour. It drew those in the Abbey and the millions outside nearer to each other than anyone else could have done.

THE MAKING OF A PRINCESS
Sandra Barwick

A confident pose in 1970, the year Diana was sent to boarding school.

The feelings of insecurity and unworthiness which haunted Diana, Princesss of Wales, throughout her life, and to which her brother was to refer in his funeral address, were rooted in her childhood. From her earliest infancy she felt that she had been a disappointment,another unwanted girl born to parents seeking a boy.

Her father, Edward John Spencer, Viscount Althorp, who was to become the 8th Earl Spencer, had desperately wanted a male heir. John, a brother born before Diana, but after her two sisters, Sarah and Jane, had died on the day of his birth in 1960. Such was the intensity of her father's longing for a boy who would keep the Spencer lands and title in his direct line that when Diana was born, on 1 July 1961, there was no girl's name prepared for her. Her christening in the church at Sandringham was quiet: there were no royal godparents, as there were to be for her younger brother, Charles, born three years later into jubilant celebration.

As children she and Charles would visit the grave of their brother who had died so quickly. If he had lived, they wondered, would either of them ever have been born? Were they, in other words, valued for themselves? Diana Spencer was to search for an answer to that question for the rest of her life.

Charles, the 9th and present Earl Spencer, has said that he believes that their mother, born Frances Roche, the younger daughter of the 4th Baron Fermoy, had been under such pressure to produce an heir, that it had helped damage her marriage.

As her daughter was to do, Frances Roche had married young and, in the eyes of society, well. At eighteen, barely out of childhood herself, she had walked up the aisle of Westminster Abbey with the heir to the Spencer title, a man many years her senior. Like her daughter, she found the fame of the family she had married into insufficient to compensate for her unhappiness in that match. When Diana was five her mother met Peter Shand Kydd, a wealthy, extrovert businessman. For the rest of her life Diana was to remember sitting on the stairs, aged six, at Park House, Sandringham, where she had been brought up from babyhood, listening to the sound of her thirty-year-old mother's footsteps going away.

It was never her mother's intention to desert her young children: she had expected, as was usual at the time, to be given custody of them. But the bitterness of the divorce, as so often in such cases, spread into a fight over the children. Frances Spencer's legal action for custody was lost after her own mother, Ruth, Lady Fermoy, appalled by what she saw as her daughter's disloyalty and lack of dutifulness in leaving her husband, gave evidence on her son-in-law's behalf. The loss of her youngest children – the elder girls were already at boarding school – was to be the mother's punishment.

The pain, guilt and anger of these traumatic events, which were fully aired in the newspapers, reverberated onto the most vulnerable parties to the actions: particularly Diana and Charles. Both were too young to understand the events which were taking place, but fully old enough to feel the atmosphere around them. In later years Diana was to say that she empathised with the rejected.

In 1969, a month after the divorce, their mother married Mr Shand Kydd and went to live with him, first in Sussex and then hundreds of miles away on the island of Seil, near Oban in Scotland. The laughter and cheerfulness their mother had brought to Park House had gone for good. Charles cried at night for his mother, and six-year-old Diana, lying awake in bed listening, castigated herself for not having the courage to go out into the dark and comfort him. Diana told a nanny early in her childhood that she was determined never to be divorced herself.

They were very lonely. In the same year as their parents' separation, Diana's elder sisters Sarah and Jane, who had fussed over their baby sister and treated her like a "living doll", were sent to boarding school. The little girl tried her best to be a mother to Charles. It was the beginning of the love of small children which was to be a striking part of her character all her life.

Unsurprisingly, Diana showed signs of tantrums, fantasy and naughtiness: throwing her clothes out of

the window, locking a nanny – from their succession of nannies – in the bathroom. Both parents tried their best, given the circumstances, to compensate the two youngest children: Johnnie Spencer coming up to the nursery to play bears on all fours and buying lavish presents. On Diana's seventh birthday her father hired a camel from a zoo for her party.

Diana loved her father, and was aware that he loved her in return. She loved her mother too, keeping a photograph of her beside her bed. Nevertheless, her upbringing, due to her birth and the divorce, was far more formal than that of most of her generation.

To be sent away from home, as a child, to school was the tradition of her class. At first she went to Silfield School, King's Lynn, but in 1970, at nine years old, Diana was sent to board at a preparatory school, Riddlesworth Hall, at Diss, Norfolk, forty miles from her home, clutching Peanuts, her favourite guinea pig, for consolation. Elisabeth Ridsdale, her headmistress, thought she was

(right) Diana at Park House, Sandringham, on her first birthday.

(below) Diana as a young child before her parents' divorce.

13

unhappy and that her work had suffered because of her parents' divorce. She was put in a special class to catch up with her peers, but never shone, though she was given a prize one year for helpfulness to others.

In 1974 she followed her mother and sisters as a boarder at a small girls' school, West Heath, near Sevenoaks, Kent. School holidays were divided between the two parents. Together, Charles and Diana "endured", in his words, the interminable train journeys between Scotland and southern England.

In the world of school too Diana felt insecure. Her brother was a very clever child: both her sisters did better academically than she did. She felt different from the rest, but seemed to shine at little except ballet, for which she grew too tall, and swimming. At West Heath she visited mentally and physically handicapped patients at a local hospital and shopped for an old lady. Her natural empathy and warmth were remarked upon. Diana was kind and unfailingly polite.

But there was no tradition in her family that girls should have academic success. Marriage, not work, was their natural end. Diana, who had low expectations of herself in the area of schoolwork, failed all five of the O-levels she took. During adolescence she found escape through cheap romances (many of them written by her future step-grandmother Barbara Cartland) about naive but pretty young girls who married princes and lived happily ever after.

Unlike most of the books' readers, she knew several princes already. At Park House she had occasionally met Prince Andrew and Prince Edward. Her sister Sarah was to go out with Prince Charles. Her maternal grandmother was Lady of the Bedchamber to the Queen Mother and her father had been equerry to George VI. Indeed, Diana's family had been aquainted with royalty for many

As a girl, Diana showed signs of a rebellious streak.

Diana with her brother Charles, now Earl Spencer. They were extremely close and Diana mothered Charles, especially after their parents' divorce.

generations. One area in which her fragile self-confidence took pride was in being a Spencer, a family settled at Althorp in Northamptonshire since 1506. She was descended on five lines, all of course illegitimate, from Charles II.

But when, in 1975, the 7th Earl Spencer, the children's grandfather, died and the family moved to the ancestral Spencer home in its 600 acres of land his children found it forbiddingly grand. When Charles in his turn inherited the title and the house, and found it still chilling, he remarked; "We never expected it to be a happy family home. It never has been."

Diana was now Lady Diana Spencer. The title did nothing to assuage her inner emptiness. The sense of alienation was increased when, a year later, Lord Spencer presented his family with a stepmother, Raine, Countess of Dartmouth, the daughter of Barbara Cartland. His children, in particular the older girls, resented her deeply, nicknaming her "Acid Raine", though Diana became reconciled to her stepmother after her father's death, remembering her devoted care of Lord Spencer after a cerebral haemorrhage came close to killing him in 1978.

At sixteen, Diana, a shy and rather awkward teenager, uneasy with her 5ft 10 height, left West Heath to spend a year preparing herself for her future role as a wife in the traditional manner of her class, at finishing school at the Institut Alpin Videmanette in Rougemont, Switzerland.

Back in London and living in her mother's house in Cadogan Place, she took a ten-week cookery course and considered training as a dance teacher. At weekends she went to her friends' country houses, and occasionally to Althorp. In 1979 she bought a flat in Coleherne Court, West London, with family funds, and found temporary work as a cleaner and a waitress. These were the years in which girls of her class marked time, waiting for a suitable marriage to come along. Diana began the search for the stable relationship which she had seen elude her parents.

With Soufflé the Shetland pony at her mother's home in Scotland in 1974.

Diana as a bridesmaid at the wedding of her sister, Lady Jane Spencer to Robert Fellowes in April 1978.

A FAIRYTALE WEDDING
Caroline Davies

The first time Lady Diana Spencer came to public attention as a potential bride for the Prince of Wales was in September 1980. A tabloid journalist, who followed the Prince's romantic attachments with a keen interest, had trained his binoculars on a heather-clad bank of the River Dee at Balmoral. He saw Prince Charles, fishing rod in hand, chasing a salmon. Then he spied a tall, fair-haired young woman watching the Prince from behind a tree.

The headlines the next day screamed "He's in Love Again" – and "Lady Di", as she became known in the popular press, became public property. In fact their serious courtship had been conducted for several months, and had been closely guarded. Indeed the Prince had known Diana Spencer for several years before their friendship became a romance.

Their first meeting was in November 1977, in the middle of a ploughed field on the Althorp estate where a shoot was in progress. Prince Charles had been romantically linked to Lady Diana's elder sister, now Lady Sarah McCorquodale, and had been invited as her guest. Lady Diana, just sixteen-years-old and attired in an unprepossessing anorak and wellingtons, had been brought along simply to make up the numbers. They seemed not to have made any impression on each other. It would, however, later be viewed as the first landmark on their road to marriage three-and-a-half years later.

Many coincidences and events drew them inexorably towards each other. In 1978 Diana's middle sister, Jane, married Sir Robert Fellowes, at that time an assistant private secretary to the Queen. This brought Lady Diana into increased contact with the Royal Family, and with the Prince of Wales in particular. She was invited to Balmoral when Sir Robert was working there.

It became a romance after an arranged meeting in July 1980. Lady Diana had just turned nineteen, and was invited to spend the weekend at a country house in Petworth, Sussex. In the evening there was a barbecue, and she found herself seated next to the Prince of Wales on a hay bale.

They talked, amongst other subjects, about the assassination, by the IRA, of Lord Mountbatten, and in a simple expression of concern that greatly

Prince Charles and Lady Diana Spencer relaxing on holiday at Balmoral.

touched the Prince, she told him how her heart had bled for him as he walked alone up the aisle at the funeral. He looked so sad, she said. It was the most tragic thing she had seen. Shortly afterwards she again found herself invited to Balmoral, but this time as the guest of the Prince himself. After their marriage he would remark that at this time: "I began to realise what was going on in my mind, and hers in particular".

Once their relationship became known to the newspapers, Lady Diana's life changed dramatically. At that time, her life revolved around a small social circle of friends, mainly made in her schooldays, and her three female flatmates. One of them, Carolyn Pride, would become Mrs Carolyn Bartholomew, and much later would play a controversial role in the dismantling of the Royal marriage. At the time of her liaison with the Prince, Diana was working as an assistant at the Young England kindergarten in Pimlico, central London.

The press seized on her suitability for the role of Princess of Wales immediately. She had the right pedigree, and with it – most assumed – the right malleability. Her physical fitness to become the mother of heirs was much commented on. There was one other qualification too. Try as they might, they could find no evidence of any previous boyfriends.

Now her flat in West London was surrounded by photographers, and the first real glimpses the world had of the future Princess, was of a young, blonde woman fleeing from cameramen on the Brompton Road, trying to get into her Mini.

She did pose for one photograph that would be reproduced a thousand times during her life. It shows her smiling nervously, with two young children from the kindergarten, her head bent in what became her trademark gesture of shyness. More significantly for the photographer she was wearing a flimsy summer skirt, which the sun streamed through, giving clear definition to the shape of her legs.

The Prince of Wales proposed in early February 1981. Days later Lady Diana slipped out of England for a holiday with her mother to Australia. On February 24, shortly after her return, Buckingham

As speculation about her relationship with the Prince grew, Diana was followed by photographers as she drove to and from work in London.

(left) The photograph which introduced the nineteen-year-old Lady Diana Spencer to the world. The impromptu photo call happened at the Young England nursery school in Pimlico, London, where Diana was working.

Palace announced: "It is with the greatest pleasure that the Queen and the Duke of Edinburgh announce the betrothal of their beloved son, the Prince of Wales, to Lady Diana Spencer, daughter of the Earl Spencer and the Honourable Mrs Shand Kydd". On that day she left her flat for the last time, with a plea to her friends: "For God's sake, ring me up – I'm going to need you". She moved to the Queen Mother's residence, Clarence House, and the preparations for the wedding were underway.

The couple posed for their official engagement photographs, and gave their first official interview together. Lady Diana was clearly besotted, her arms around her husband and her sapphire and diamond engagement ring on display on the third finger of her left hand. She was, she said, looking forward to being "a good wife", and thought her life ahead would be "challenging". The Prince quipped: "She will keep me young" – alluding to the twelve - year age gap that had attracted some comment. When asked if they were in love, Lady Diana responded "Of course". Her future husband added "Whatever love is" – a remark that would be dissected and analysed in years to come.

At her first official outing with her fiancé the world saw a dramatic change of image for a woman who had hitherto dressed conservatively. She arrived at Goldsmith's Hall in a décolleté black taffeta dress – a considerable contrast to her formerly discreet image. The impact that dress made heralded her role as a fashion icon, and caused the octogenarian Lady Diana Cooper to quip: "Wasn't that a mighty

(left) The engagement of the Prince of Wales and Lady Diana Spencer was announced on 24 February 1981. They appeared on the steps of Buckingham Palace to pose for photographers.

(right) An official engagement photograph by Snowdon.

feast to set before a King?".

The wedding, on a gloriously hot day on July 29 1981, was a fairytale occasion, on which, according to the vast crowds that gathered, it seemed all the hopes of the nation were pinned. Lady Diana was descended from the Stuart Kings, Charles II and James II. She would return this line to the Royal Family through her sons. She herself was Prince Charles's seventh cousin once removed. It meant his heirs could claim lineage from every English king who had left descendants.

A national holiday was declared. Many heads of state attended, including nearly all the crowned heads of Europe. A congregation of 2,500 gathered at St Paul's Cathedral, while television cameras conveyed the ceremony to an estimated 750 million across the globe – the largest television audience recorded at that time.

Her journey up the long aisle at St Paul's Cathedral was highly charged and emotional as she walked on the arm of her father, Earl Spencer, frail after a near fatal brain haemorrhage. Her ivory silk dress, designed by David and Elizabeth Emanuel, lavish in detail with a magnificent lengthy train, drew gasps.

The Archbishop of Canterbury, Dr Robert Runcie, referred to it as "the stuff of which fairytales are made". Three orchestras played, and Kiri te Kanawa – soon afterwards appointed Dame – sang. Diana had chosen her favourite school hymn "I vow to thee my Country". It combined the pageantry of a State occasion with the simplicity of a private wedding.

Given the atmosphere, it was hardly surprising that the shy and nervous bride stumbled on her vows, mixing up her husband's name and saying: "I take thee Philip Charles Arthur George to be my wedded husband".

Later at Buckingham Palace, Diana, now Her Royal Highness the Princess of Wales, appeared on the balcony with her husband and their families. The couple's kiss drew roars of approval from the crowd of thousands gathered below. "What an unbelievable day it was", the Prince later remarked.

The first night of their honeymoon was spent at Broadlands, the Mountbatten estate in Hampshire and a favourite retreat for Prince Charles. There followed a two-week Mediterranean cruise aboard the Royal Yacht *Britannia*. The couple returned to the royal family's Scottish retreat at Balmoral, where they stayed until mid-September.

Three years after they had first met, and three weeks after her 20th birthday, Lady Diana Spencer became the first Princess of Wales for 71 years, and the third lady of Great Britain, following in order of precedence only the Queen and the Queen Mother.

With the Queen after the Privy Council had granted the couple permission to marry.

(right) Diana arriving with her father at St Paul's Cathedral on her wedding day, 29 July 1981.

(below) Diana at the altar with her father and Prince Charles.

(Overleaf) An informal moment backstage at
Buckingham Palace with Her Majesty the Queen
and bridesmaids.

Now man and wife, the couple travel in a state landau from
St Paul's Cathedral to Buckingham Palace.

(Right) The kiss on the balcony at Buckingham Palace,
watched by a crowd of thousands.

The honeymooners break off to pose for the cameras on the
banks of the Dee at Balmoral.

Waving goodbye to Gibraltar from the Royal Yacht *Britannia*
on their honeymoon cruise.

PRINCESS AND MOTHER
Elizabeth Grice

The princess and her sons photographed by one of Diana's favourite photographers, Patrick Demarchelier.

At some time or other, self-doubt assailed Diana, Princess of Wales, in every department of her personal and public life except one: she knew she was a good mother. This was the only tribute that really mattered to her.

Beyond people believing in the sincerity of her work for worthwhile causes, beyond winning the warmth of her public or being understood after her marriage disintegrated, Diana wished to demonstrate that in the imperfect art of parenthood, she had done everything in her power to succeed.

In this she was guided by two principles. She clung to the belief that her sons should be brought up as normally as possible despite the demands of an abnormal destiny and she wanted to bestow on them the unselfconscious affection, warmth and stability that had been lacking both in her own childhood and in that of the Prince of Wales.

Her first pregnancy came so quickly after her marriage that she had barely begun to get used to being a wife before she was trying to come to terms with the fact that she was soon to be a mother.

The birth of Prince William on June 21, 1982, came after a long and difficult labour, at which Prince Charles was present in the Lindo wing of St Mary's Hospital, Paddington, West London. Prince Charles asked the crowd which had gathered with champagne outside the hospital to quieten down: "Sleep is badly needed." A courtier observed, "She has done well, producing a boy first time." Royal protocol was observed to celebrate the heir's birth: a forty-one-gun salute in Hyde Park and another at the Tower of London.

Less than twenty-four hours later Diana, who had chosen to breastfeed the baby, returned to Kensington Palace. Barbara Barnes was hired as nanny to the Prince, nick-named "Wills" by his mother who had chosen his first name. The prince was christened on 4 August 1982, howling loudly when he saw the cameras which were to record the event.

On her public engagements, which Diana resumed some months after the birth, she talked about him to the crowd: "I always find time each day for William; he comes first ... always."

The next year she was allowed to take the nine-

month-old Prince William with her and Prince Charles on a highly successful six-week tour of Australia and New Zealand, where the spotlight never left her. In private she wept with nerves, in public she appeared to glow with happiness and excitement. Crowds on the side of the road which Prince Charles walked down groaned in disappointment. He commented that he should have had two wives.

In Australia the Princess of Wales again talked about her feelings for her son. When a woman in Canberra holding a fractious baby said she wished she had a nanny too, Diana replied: "I would swop with you any time. I wish I didn't have to leave William with a nanny. I would rather do what you are doing."

However, in June 1983 Prince William was left behind while his parents visited Canada for two weeks, missing his first birthday. Despite her evident popularity, the Princess continued to find the pressures of her position hard.

Hours after her arrival in Nova Scotia she told a woman in the crowds waiting to see her: "I wish I had William with me. We've only been away a few hours, but I miss him very much. I'm really sorry we couldn't bring him."

Later, in an interview Prince Charles said that he and the Princess intended to bring up their children: "to be well mannered, to think of other people, to put themselves into other people's positions".

In 1984, after a series of false warnings in the newspapers, the Princess was pregnant again. On 15 September Prince Harry was born, later described by her as: "an extraordinarily good baby". This time the roar from the crowd outside St Mary's hospital when the announcement was made was so loud that someone nearby drove into the side of an ambulance.

His hair was "an indeterminate colour", Prince Charles, who again had been present at the birth, said. It was in fact a typical Spencer red, described by him in private as "rusty". Prince William was, his father later revealed, a little jealous at Prince Harry's arrival. He was christened on 21 December.

The Princess of Wales had now fulfilled the unspoken part of her wedding contract, producing,

(right) Diana on a walkabout in May 1982 – her last official engagement before the birth of Prince William.

(below) Diana looks on fondly as her husband gives a speech at the Royal Academy.

as she dubbed them "the heir and the spare". Remembering her mother's experience, she later remarked, "It would have been a little tricky if it had been two girls."

The Prince and Princess of Wales retained two nannies, one full-time nanny, living in at Kensington Palace, and one for weekends at Highgrove. Though there were rumours, and occasionally reports, that something was wrong with their marriage, most royal watchers concentrated their enthusiasm on Diana's changing hairstyles, with occasional revelations that the couple were "royal lovebirds" and that Prince Charles was busy changing nappies and cooking leek and noodle casserole at Highgrove.

Suggestions that the Princess, whose weight visibly fluctuated, was suffering from anorexia were specifically denied by the Palace, which said that she was simply a keen fan of Jane Fonda's exercise programme.

In the years that followed Diana was to see her marriage fall apart. But in her bleakest moments within the royal establishment, her sons were a constant reminder to her that, in one area at least, she had not failed. She wanted to bring them up to be able to cope with a role she herself, and to some extent her husband, had found so hard.

"I want them to have an understanding of people's emotions, of people's insecurities, of people's distress, of their hopes and dreams," she said in answer to suggestions that Princes William and Harry were too young to be introduced to hostels for the homeless and to AIDS sufferers. Later, in her interview for the *Panorama* programme for BBC television, there was a hint both of pride and of defiance that these were places where "no one of that age in this family has been before". By showing them lives so far removed from their own, she

hoped to offer an antidote to privilege.

Diana was determined to be intimately involved in her sons' upbringing. In the early days of parenthood and within the confines of the royal schedule, both she and the Prince of Wales tried hard to be models of involvement with their children. But as their marriage ran into difficulties, two apparently different styles of parenting were seized on by the press.

Diana took them to fast food restaurants in Kensington, and Happy Eaters on the A1 on the way back to London from Sandringham. She ran barefoot in a parents' race at the school sports day, and was pictured in a baseball cap, wet and laughing, on a white-knuckle theme-park ride; Charles was shown stiffly introducing his sons to the tweedy, country pursuits he preferred.

Although the polarity in their approaches may sometimes have been misleading, there is no doubt

(left) Posing for a photograph to celebrate their first wedding anniversary, the Prince and Princess of Wales take the opportunity to show off Prince William, born 21 June 1982.

A natural family portrait at Kensington Palace with Prince William aged six months.

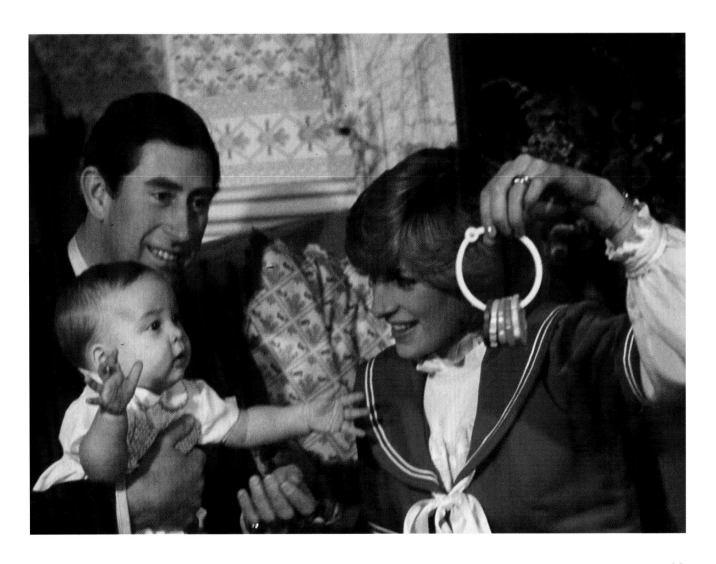

that Diana – "leading from the heart, not the head," as she once said – possessed the ability to be an openly affectionate and spontaneous mother to an unusual degree.

"It is important not to underestimate the value of simple things – hugs for example," she told a charity gathering. "Hugs can do a great amount of good – especially for children."

It was largely at Diana's insistence that William and Harry should not be educated, even from primary-school age, in the confines of a royal palace as their father had been, but at Ludgrove Preparatory School and then at Eton. She believed that contact with children of the Princes' own age in a reasonably normal environment was the best possible preparation for a balanced future.

Worried that Prince Harry, as the second son, would be made to feel an also-ran by comparison with his elder brother, she insisted that no difference should be made between them.

To the inescapable official schooling of Prince William in the burdens of monarchy, Diana lent her own intuitive ideas about compassion and responsibility.

She was a fiercely protective mother, worrying ceaselessly about the effects of media intrusion on the lives of her sons – and yet, paradoxically, responsible for a good deal of it. The Princes had to weather many difficult revelations about their parents' marriage but Diana was on hand to see them through each crisis. They, in turn, were what a friend called her "loving lifeline".

In the months before her death, the Princess's comments about how the future would turn out for her sons were edged with caution. Only time would tell, she said. Their ability to cope and to mature without her will be the greatest testimony to their mother's influence.

(left) Portrait of a young mother: this formal study by Snowdon marked the princess's 21st birthday, only ten days after the birth of Prince William.

Diana chats to girls after they had danced for her at the Ethnic Cultural Centre during her visit to Handsworth, Birmingham, December 1982.

Popular at home and abroad: Diana on a walkabout
in Tauranga on the royal tour to New Zealand in 1983.

(below) Leaving the Lindo wing of St Mary's Paddington with Prince Harry, born 15 September 1984.

(right) A comforting hug. Diana bestowed on her children the affection and warmth that had been lacking in her own childhood.

(below) The family on holiday in 1985.

Escorting the young Prince William to his first day at nursery school in September 1985. The princess preferred taking an active part in her children's lives to allowing nannies full-time responsibility for their care.

(overleaf) Causing a stir by dancing with Wayne Sleep.

THE PRINCESS OF STYLE
Hilary Alexander

In the poignant reworking of his song, 'Candle in the Wind', Elton John sang in tribute to Diana, Princess of Wales, as "England's Rose". It is a phrase that pierced the soul of a grieving nation; an informal title which captured her many gifts, her frailty, vulnerability and beauty. Yet her appeal as a fashion figurehead lay, ultimately, in its very antithesis of so-called English style.

She was an international icon, an ambassadress who turned the concept of royal fashion upside down. She banished the stiff formality of the taffeta-and-tiara era, ushering in a fresh, youthful antidote to the frumpy, regulation "occasion wear" we had come to associate with the older Windsor women.

In newspapers, magazines and on television, we watched her progress over sixteen years, like a butterfly emerging from a chrysalis. Before our eyes, she was transformed from a shy, plump teenager, the Sloane Ranger in identikit pie-crust-frill blouses, lumpy sweaters and long, gathered skirts to become the most photographed woman in the world; the symbol of international glamour whose every nuance was watched and admired.

The transformation was not without its hitches. Some early outfits were over-fussy, as Diana struggled to dress for the first role the public bestowed upon her as "fairy princess". She looked back on those years as her "early fairy period". Other ensembles were alarmingly patterned, hectically coloured or of curious cut. But they were always different.

When she wore hats, she revitalised a moribund British industry, inspiring a new generation of milliners. When she wore jewellery – a diamanté lizard from Butler & Wilson, for example, or Queen Mary's diamond and emerald choker as a Charleston-style headband – she sparked trends.

She pioneered the column gown, shimmering with pearls and beads. It was often one-shouldered, sometimes almost backless or with its own matching bolero jacket – a Catherine Walker signature. With its long, sinuous silhouette, it was light years removed from the full-skirted "meringue" previously associated with royal galas.

We were intrigued by her because here was a truly independent fashion personality in the making,

Diana was the first person to wear a *haute couture* gown from British designer John Galliano's collection for Christian Dior in 1996.

genetically blessed with the looks, the legs and the figure of a supermodel. Allied to an instinctive compassion and a natural, the combination was potent and irresistible.

Diana wore British designers, championing many of those who are now household names – Bruce Oldfield, the Emanuels, Zandra Rhodes, Jasper Conran, Bella Pollen, Christina Stambolian, Roland Klein, Victor Edelstein, Bellville Sassoon, Murray Arbeid, Jacques Azagury, Tomasz Starzewski, and, most enduringly, Catherine Walker, who designed the formal black dress she was buried in. But hers was not British style.

She wore designs by the late Gianni Versace, Valentino, Giorgio Armani, Escada and Mondi, Karl Lagerfeld for Chanel, Christian Lacroix and John Galliano for Christian Dior. Yet she never followed a Euro-fashion line.

Off-duty with her sons she wore jeans, sweatshirts, baseball caps and loafers; she worked out, swam and in-line skated until her muscle tone was taut and her skin glowed. But her old-fashioned charm sparkled as much as the veneer of streamlined 90s woman.

Years of living in the limelight gave her an understanding of the power of clothes and the emotions they can convey, which she used to maximum advantage. But she had, too, an intuitive sense of how to dress for the job whether she was dancing with John Travolta at the White House, visiting a hospital in Lahore in traditional *shalwar khameez*, or talking to war victims in Angola or Bosnia to publicise the horror of landmines.

Her campaign against landmines proved her determination to be seen as something more than a "clothes-horse", a decision signalled by the charity auction of 79 of her gowns from her in June, 1997.

In the weeks before her death, evening appearances had seen her wearing the short, sparkly, cleavage-enhancing sheaths and higher heels which proclaimed her liberation and new-found sensuality, while her working wardrobe was honed to blazer, T-shirt and chinos or open-necked shirt and jeans. But it did not really matter what she wore, she was always distinctive.

Her style was hers – every look she made her own.

(right) Staying loyal to the designers of her wedding dress, Diana wears a beaded Emanuel dress for a modern regal look.

Wearing Bellville Sassoon during her "early fairy period", and (below) the Emanuels again for a gala at the Royal Opera House in 1988.

Catherine Walker helped Diana to establish her personal style and became a confidant and friend. (left) In peppermint green silk by Catherine Walker for a film premier in London, and (below) in a Grace Kelly inspired dress by the same designer.

Demonstrating the versatility of her style in (below left) a Catherine Walker tuxedo and a Hackett green silk waistcoat, and (below) in a Pakistani-inspired outfit by the same designer.

The one-shouldered look was a Diana favourite:
(right) by Hachi, and (far right) by Gina Fratelli for Hartnell.

Favouring British designers: Diana wears (left) Bruce
Oldfield, and (below) Rifat Ozbek with her friend Elton
John.

(right) On overseas trips, Diana had to take local conditions into account. She wore long skirts to Arab states, more casual clothes for hot climates and even traditional dress for her private visit to Pakistan in 1997.

While many of her official functions demanded splendid evening gowns, Diana's work also required a more practical approach to dressing. She was a trendsetter by day and by night as these photographs show.

As Diana's global celebrity grew, so did the international nature of her wardrobe. Wearing (below left) Versace and (below right) Lacroix in Paris.

(right) On the evening that Prince Charles admitted adultery on national television, Diana arrived at the Serpentine Gallery in London's Hyde Park looking stunning in a Christina Stambolian dress.

PUBLIC SMILES, PRIVATE SORROWS
Caroline Davies

The public adored the Princess of Wales. Her presence electrified the crowds. Behind her dazzling smile, however, she was in turmoil and finding her marriage and the profile it brought with it increasingly intolerable. The cracks, it would emerge, were there long before their behaviour in public gave any indication that theirs was anything other than the fairytale marriage the nation had so hoped for.

When she gave birth to Prince William on 21 June 1982, the photograph of mother and father looking adoringly at their first-born belied the real unhappiness she was experiencing. Years later she would admit that she was unable to come to terms with her role, had no idea what it should be, and found little solace from the people she turned to for help – namely her husband and the Palace courtiers. Although she appeared radiant when carrying out her official duties, often she was in tears as she and the Prince of Wales travelled to venues, pleading that she could not cope.

In January 1982, while four months pregnant, she fell down a staircase at Sandringham in front of the Queen Mother. It was later claimed this was a half-hearted suicide attempt, a claim she was later to give credibility to. After the birth she suffered post-natal depression, something which she felt the royal family were unable to understand, and became thin, pale and withdrawn. Apart from her physical appearance, there was nothing else to indicate that the marriage was in jeopardy.

Her depression worsened after the birth of Prince Harry in September 1984, manifesting itself in the form of the disease *Bulimia nervosa*, a psychiatric illness where feelings of unworthiness lead to sufferers bingeing on food then vomiting it up. In the Panorama interview she explained: "It was a symptom of what was going on in my marriage. I was crying out for help, but giving all the wrong signals and people were using my bulimia as a coat on a hanger. They decided that was the problem – Diana was unstable."

It was on a sunshine holiday in the summer of 1986 that the first hint of tension in their marriage became evident. Prince Charles came home three days early from Majorca, leaving his wife behind

Diana on the royal tour of Korea in 1992. Photographs from the tour told the world that the marriage between the Prince and Princess of Wales was over.

with their sons, then aged four and two. Her husband's early departure set a pattern that was to become familiar over the next six years. The following year, at a polo match, when Charles went to kiss her for consolation after losing she wiped her lips with the back of her hand. No one knew then, but she had already begun her friendship with Captain James Hewitt, which would eventually turn into an adulterous affair.

Despite the private domestic separation, the couple believed it was possible that they could continue to appear in public together, which they did. However, the rift became even more obvious when in 1987 the Prince spent more than one month at Balmoral while she and the children remained at Kensington Palace. Such a long time apart prompted speculation and comment about a possible split. Official spokesmen were forced into

making the excuse – albeit feeble – that the Prince was extremely busy managing the estate.

On his return, the roadshow continued, and both were persuaded to visit homes in West Wales which had been severely damaged by flooding. Alas, their behaviour did nothing to quell the rumours. They arrived separately, departed separately, for different destinations, and in the few hours they spent together were not observed to have exchanged one single word. Their marriage would never recover.

They spent more and more time apart, he burying himself at Highgrove where he mixed socially with his circle of friends including Camilla Parker-Bowles, with whom he was to have an adulterous affair. His friends did not appeal to the Princess, who disliked polo and country pursuits. Her friends were bewildering to the Prince, who was not at home at a disco, or even a dance floor. She liked the pop

group Dire Straits, and he preferred Berlioz.

The death of Major Hugh Lindsay in the Klosters skiing avalanche, in which the Prince narrowly escaped death or serious injury, was a turning point for the Princess. It was 1988, and the shock of the tragedy forced her to confront the flaws in her own life and attempt to do something about the nervous ailments that had plagued her. She sought medical help and counselling.

Even at this point, when things were going so disastrously, they sought to present a united front in public. But increasingly they found it difficult to conceal in public what was happening in private. In 1990 on a tour of the Cameroons, the Prince and Princess sat apart for photographs, looking in opposite directions. Again they left separately, he to go sketching in Tunisia, and she to fly back to Kensington Palace. By then Diana's relationship with

(left) The 1985 tour to America. Observers noticed how thin the Princess looked and concerns were raised about her health.

(below) Dancing with John Travolta, with the President and Mrs Reagan looking on, during a reception at the White House.

Hewitt became the focus of speculative reports on the state of the marriage in March 1991. Still they continued their official relationship, visiting Czechoslovakia – albeit staying in separate rooms. A few months later, the Princess declined to celebrate her 30th birthday party at Highgrove, although she did join her husband on a cruise of the Mediterranean.

Perhaps the most public indication she gave of their distance was on their trip to India in February 1992. It was on the eve of St Valentine's and at the end of a polo match in which Prince Charles played in Jaipur. The Princess presented the prizes. As he went to kiss her – for the first time in public for four years – she turned her head at the very last moment. In full view of all the photographers, he tried to follow her round with his lips, and almost lost his balance. All his lips found was her ear, and there was an earring in the way. The pictures were used in almost every newspaper as confirmation that their love – if it had ever existed – had totally withered. If that were not evidence enough, the Princess allowed herself to be photographed alone, in front of the Taj Mahal, a shrine to marital love. Three months later she made a solo visit to Egypt, and was once again pictured alone in the desert in front of the Giza pyramids. Her undeniable message was clear.

She began to develop her own interests, and concentrated on charities that reflected her connection with the neglected, and those with feelings of inadequacy. Inspired by a private meeting with Mother Teresa, she envisaged a role for herself which was not dependent on her marriage.

If there had, by that stage, been any chance of reconciliation, it was damned by the publication in June 1992 of Andrew Morton's book *Diana, her true story*. It revealed to the public a very different Princess to the one they had seen at the side of her husband. It contained the explosive claims she suffered from bulimia, and had made suicide attempts. It portrayed Diana as lonely and neurotic,

A semblance of unity in a family portrait by Snowdon, taken in 1991 at the Prince's Gloucestershire estate, Highgrove.

and Charles as a distant father and uncaring husband. Doubts about the origins of the book were squashed when, three days after the initial extracts were published, the Princess paid a high-profile visit to Carolyn Bartholomew, godmother to Prince Harry and one of the book's main contributors.

The following month saw the Princess again at Balmoral, and also the publication of the text of an intimate telephone conversation between her and James Gilbey, in which he referred to her as "Squidgy" and blew kisses down the line. Still the public facade was maintained. Diana accompanied Prince Charles on a four-day visit to Korea. They looked so ill at ease, and so miserable, that the journalists accompanying the tour dubbed them "The Glums". While they were there, there were allegations made that the Duke of Edinburgh had written to her reproaching her for her behaviour. On her return to Britain, her office at Kensington Palace issued an unprecedented statement denying the claims. The Prince, by then in Hong Kong, endorsed her statement.

The situation was by now intolerable. There could be no concealing the fact that there was no longer any marriage to retrieve. On 9th December, 1992, the then Prime Minister John Major announced to a packed House of Commons something almost everyone already knew. The Prince and Princess of Wales had agreed to separate. It ended a year, described by the Queen as her *annus horribilis*.

Then in 1993 further damage was caused by the publication of an intimate phone conversation between the Prince and Mrs Parker-Bowles, and at the end of the year the Princess made the dramatic and tearful television announcement that she planned to bow out of public life and drop most of her charity patronages. It was a purely temporary move, and soon she was seen at events promoting the causes she espoused: care for those suffering from leprosy, AIDS, the homeless. She was carving a role she felt suited her, and would continue to do so. The separation had done nothing to diminish her public profile, indeed it appeared to enhance it.

If the royal family had hoped the separation could be managed with dignity, their hopes were shattered when the broadcaster Jonathan Dimbleby

(top left) Talking to a patient at the London Lighthouse AIDS Centre in July 1992. Diana's acceptance of people with the HIV virus and AIDS caused an international change in attitudes. She was not afraid to be seen touching or hugging sufferers.

(bottom left) A welcoming crowd outside a residential and training centre for the blind in Leatherhead, Surrey in January 1995.

(below) Diana was a keen dancer as a child but grew too tall to become a professional herself. She was patron of the English National Ballet and is seen here chatting to ballet students in 1988.

published his biography of the Prince of Wales. It was accompanied by a television interview with Prince Charles in which he admitted committing adultery after it was clear his marriage had irretrievably broken down. It ensured that their partnership ended in a fiasco of biographies and interviews which made divorce inevitable.

Now there were claims – undisputed – that the Prince had never loved his wife, and proposed to her only because his father had bullied him into it. It was becoming clear that the marriage was problematic before it even began. Publicity continued to attend the Princess, and she was photographed holidaying in Martha's Vineyard, looking drawn and thin, still searching for an identity.

She retaliated with breathtaking candour in the interview for the BBC's *Panorama* programme, recorded on 5th November, 1995, and broadcast on November 20th. She revealed her misery and her wrath. She spelt out the role she wanted to fulfil, as an ambassador for Great Britain around the world, and as the "queen of people's hearts". She also made it clear that she would fight for her children and had no intention of initiating a divorce.

But four weeks later, dismayed by the now public nature of the marriage's disintegration, the Queen wrote to her son and daughter-in-law urging a quick divorce in order the spare the feelings of the children.

In February 1996 she brokered a deal at a tea-time summit alone with her husband in his apartments at St James's Palace, and afterwards telephoned the Queen to ask for an announcement. On 15th July, the Prince was granted a *decree nisi*, made absolute at 10.27 a.m. on 28th August. At the time the Prince was at Balmoral with Princes William and Harry. The Princess was at the studios of the English National Ballet in London. The third finger of her left hand said it all. She was still deliberately wearing the sapphire and diamond cluster engagement ring that the Prince had bought for her.

At a refugee camp in Zimbabwe 1993.

(right) Diana covers her ears during an RAF fly past.

(below) Inspecting the parade of the second battalion of the Queen's and Royal Hampshires' presentation of colours at Howe Barracks in Canterbury in May 1995.

(left) On a visit to India, Diana was captured sitting alone contemplating the Taj Mahal, a monument to one man's love for his wife. The image spoke volumes about the state of the Wales's marriage.

(right) Diana turns from Charles as he kisses her after a polo match in Jaipur, India in 1992.

(below) The miserable couple on the tour to Korea were nicknamed "The Glums". Their official separation was announced only months later.

After their separation, the Prince and Princess appeared together with their sons at official functions or on family occasions. (right) At the VJ-Day celebrations in 1995 and (below) on Prince William's first day at Eton.

At all times, the Princess combined her official duties with being a mother: (top left) giving a tired Prince Harry a piggyback after a polo match and (bottom left) rushing to embrace Prince William as she boards the Royal Yacht *Britannia* to join her children during a visit to Canada in October 1991.

Diana tried to show her sons sides of life which they might not have otherwise seen: (below) laughing after a drenching at Thorpe Park in 1992.

DIANA, PRINCESS OF WALES
W. F. Deedes

In the year before her death, Diana had started to carve out a new role for herself. She pruned the number of charities she was involved with and concentrated on working with six of the causes closest to her heart. One of these was the anti-landmine campaign and she can be seen here giving a speech in Luanda, Angola in January 1997.

In the year after her divorce and the last year of her life, Diana, Princess of Wales, devoted herself to working for those causes dearest to her heart. Shortly before she died, I travelled with her to Bosnia.

We had first discussed this Bosnia trip early in 1997 before she made an expedition to Angola to publicise the damage landmines had done to that country. It had been a subject of concern to me from the early 1990s. Travelling in Asia and Africa to write about famine, refugees and other crises, I saw what a deadly enemy mines had become to some of the poorest people on Earth. Diana shared that concern. Furthermore, she emphasised to me, her concern about mines and their victims would continue. Angola was not, she insisted, to be seen as a one-off. Where next?

I suggested Bosnia was her best bet. For if you are going to concern yourself with the consequences of man's inhumanity to man as closely as Diana desired to do, Sarajevo is the place to go. On our first day we had no time to stop there, because of engagements in Tuzla, which was a long drive away. So we drove straight through the city, past its huge cemeteries, up what was called Sniper's Alley, through streets of shattered offices and homes. Mostly we sat in silence, as she looked around her, taking it in, saying nothing, betraying no emotion.

Part of her gift in bringing comfort to those in anguish, I came to learn, lay in this sensitive awareness of when silence is best. She was not a voluble sympathiser, quite the reverse. At some point during an outpouring of grief, she would stretch out a hand or both hands and touch the person on the arm or face.

I found some of the tales we had to hear almost unendurable. Yet I never saw her lose this calm, which plainly had a most soothing effect. As I reported at the time, she saw dreadful wounds, heard horrifying stories while maintaining the demeanour of a professional but sympathetic nurse. Nor in the course of those three days did I see her concentration flag; and this was remarkable because the distractions were intense. The camera crews and the reporters who met her at every stop had an interest in her encounters with victims of

(below and left) As a volunteer for the British Red Cross Anti Landmine Campaign Diana wears protective clothing to walk through a recently cleared landmine field in Angola.

mines, but, unlike the Angolan expedition, it was not their main interest. She had, as it later transpired, interrupted her holiday to visit Bosnia. Much of the holiday was spent with Dodi Fayed. The pictures were public. Therein lay the main press interest. It was a test of temper, of temperament and of character.

She would utter a faint murmur of dismay at the sight of forty photographers lined up outside some humble home. Then self-discipline would assert itself. It afforded an opportunity to witness, at uncomfortably close range, the dichotomy of Diana's attitude to photographers. Defending their profession, some of them claim she was hopelessly inconsistent in her attitude to the camera. She resented their presence, so the argument goes, yet depended upon their work for the standing it gave her and her causes.

Our expedition helped me to reach a conclusion about this. She accepted the value of photographers in her life, and acknowledged the inestimable value they held for her good causes. What she found harder to stomach was the intrusive lengths to which some, in such an intensely competitive game, were ready to go and sought to take her.

It was the unknown and the unexpected which troubled her. It is hardly a human aberration to resent being spied upon by hidden cameras.

The emotional encounters we had with victims and the bereaved left their mark on her. What often seemed a calm, soothing response to a tale of woe took more of a toll than one at first supposed. She made it hard for herself, insisting that every interview be granted at least thirty minutes. What made it even harder was the depths of bitterness sown by this civil war in former Yugoslavia. "So many people," I said to her at one point, "long to find someone who will listen while they express their inner feelings about all this – and they've found you." Sad smile. No response.

Instead, she asked me which of the interviews during the day I felt had been the most emotional. We agreed on the answer. It had been a meeting with a young Muslim widow whose husband had been killed by a mine while he was fishing a few months before. The widow sat on one side of the

Princess, the man's mother on the other.

The mother told us how she had been with her son in hospital, "as he died, smiling". The widow spoke of their short but happy marriage, and described him simply as a good man, an honest man, concluding: "And he was only twenty-nine when he died."

Diana said very little. She caught up both their hands and held them. The mother explained her dream. In this, she told us, her son had returned to her, and explained that he was happy where he was. "That might well be so," Diana responded. It seemed at the time a perfect rejoinder. The mother's face was transformed.

There was a similar encounter in one of Sarajevo's largest cemeteries. The Princess went off alone to walk round it. As she did so, she encountered a mother tending her son's grave. There was no language barrier. The two women gently embraced. Watching this scene from a distance, I sought in my mind who else could have done this. Nobody.

"I am a humanitarian. I always have been, and I always will be," she declared within my hearing during the Angola expedition when they accused her of meddling in politics. In saying that, she wrote her own epitaph, for that, I came to learn, was what she really thought about herself. Yet nobody could write about Diana, as I sometimes had to do, without being made aware of the passions which swirled around her, and will go on swirling.

She had her critics, and even in death she will continue to have them. It does her memory no service to brush that aside. There were two Dianas; and sometimes one of them appeared to conflict with the best interests of the other.

All that said, it is surely right to dwell on the supreme quality of one who sought above all to help the vulnerable people in society, and who did it so well. She was good at this because she herself was vulnerable. She knew the feeling. She did not set out to be a saint.

This was a human being, with all the faults of most of us, but also with a bigger heart than most of us. As I discovered on that last mission for humanity, there was an underlying humility which, at least to

(above and right)To publicise the plight of landmine victims, Diana visits the Kikolo health post in the slums of Luanda, Angola.

me, redeems it all.

She was not a grand person setting out to bestow favours on the poor. She knew herself too well for that. Recognising her own frailty, she was the better able to understand and to sympathise with the frailty of others. As I perceived in Bosnia, she saw herself as an equal with those she sought to comfort. That was part of her gift. As she told *Le Monde*: "To begin with we are on the same level, on the same wavelength." That is why she could sit in absolute silence, holding a hand, and transmit a feeling of "we're in this together".

To have witnessed the way she brought comfort to those people, many in deep distress, some in tears is to understand what we have lost, for ever.

More simply, Diana gave us an example, in this mechanistic world, which we should heed and try never to forget. Her instinct was so right: all those wounded people in Bosnia, crying aloud for someone to hear their tale, to hold their hand, to be able to communicate the uncommunicable.

We should tell our children and our grandchildren about her. We should say to them, the world you are about to enter remains in sore need of her gifts. Remember her.

(Right) Diana poses with the children of landmine victim Muhamed Soljankic in Tuzla, Bosnia in early August 1997.

(left) Taking part in a meeting on landmines with Elizabeth Dole, President of the American Red Cross, in June 1997.

(above) At a cemetery in Sarajevo, Diana comforts a local resident grieving for her son who was killed in the war.

(left) Sharing a joke with French NATO soldiers in Sarajevo, Bosnia, in August 1997.

On a visit to Pakistan with her friend, Jemima Khan in February 1997. With a young cancer patient, they enjoy a show by patients at the Shaukat Khanum Memorial Cancer Hospital in Lahore.

Still attracting crowds overseas, despite losing her royal
title, Diana shakes hands outside the Victor Chang Cardiac
Institute in Sydney, Australia in November 1996.

The family reunites for Prince William's confirmation
at Windsor Castle in March 1997.

A new image for a new life: (below) Diana sits for Mario Testino and features on the cover of *Vanity Fair*, and (right) models a daring Versace dress at the Tate in August 1997.

(Far right) Sprinting to her car after a regular morning session at her gym in West London. The Princess was naturally athletic and enjoyed dancing, swimming and playing tennis.

THE NATION MOURNS
Colin Randall

Soon after the news of Diana's death broke, the public began laying flowers at the royal palaces. A policeman carries flowers from the public to lay alongside the funeral route on 6 September 1997.

The sense of unreality began with the official radio announcement, in the early hours of Sunday 31 August 1997, that Diana, Princess of Wales was dead, followed, eerily, by "God Save the Queen".

Then and, as so many were to find, for days afterwards, it seemed too much to take in: the Princess with Dodi Fayed, her close companion through the all too well documented recent past, were dead after a car crash that had occurred as they were pursued by paparazzi through the centre of one of the world's most romantic cities.

At first, that was the sole bleak fact and news organisations struggled to find ways to flesh the story out, to help make it more believable for their audience, for themselves. The stunned shock of anyone available for a quote on the last day of the silly season was recorded.

The role of the press in the Princess's life and death was uppermost in the mind of her younger brother, Earl Spencer, as he addressed the press from outside his Cape Town home.

"I always believed the Press would kill her in the end," he said with undisguised bitterness. "But not even I could imagine that they would take such a direct hand in her death, as seems to be the case. It will appear that every proprietor and editor of every publication that has paid for intrusive and exploitative photographs of her, encouraging greedy and ruthless individuals to risk everything in pursuit of Diana's image, has blood on his hands today."

Though anger coloured a brother's reaction, it was incredulousness and a sense of personal loss which characterised the reactions of countless ordinary citizens who made their way to the royal households of England and Scotland, and to Harrods, owned by Dodi's father, bearing flowers.

The anguish of the Princess's sons, Princes William and Harry, roused during the night by their father with whom they were holidaying at Balmoral, to be told the awful news, was felt with special keenness.

Tony Blair, the Prime Minister, paused on his way to church with his own family in his constituency to offer a tribute that articulated the nation's mood.

"I feel like everyone else in this country," he said. "I am utterly devastated. [The Princess was a] wonderful and warm human being, although her

life was often sadly touched by tragedy ... she was the People's Princess and that is how she will remain in our hearts and our memories forever."

Before Sunday was over, the Prince of Wales had flown to Paris with the Princess's sisters, Lady Jane Fellowes and Lady Sarah McCorquodale, to collect the coffin containing the body of his former wife, and bring it home to RAF Northolt, west of London. The simple, moving reception, televised to the country, somehow made the incredible news real.

As flowers piled higher outside the Princess's home, Kensington Palace, and people gathered in long queues outside St James's Palace, where her body lay in rest, to sign books of condolence, Buckingham Palace began discussions with the Spencer family and 10 Downing Street, under the direction of Lt.-Col. Malcolm Ross, Comptroller of the Lord Chamberlain's Office.

A State ceremony was ruled out in favour of an occasion designed as "a unique funeral for a unique person", blending pomp and charity and modernity in a fitting tribute to an exceptional life.

On the eve of the funeral, the Queen, in what the *Daily Telegraph* described as the most remarkable and personal message of her reign, went on live television to urge her people to "show to the whole world the British nation united in grief". She said she joined the nation in its determination to cherish the Princess's memory.

Earlier the same day, the young Princes had arrived in London from Balmoral and travelled with their father to their mother's home, Kensington Palace. There, in brief televised scenes that tore at the hearts of millions, they accepted mourners' messages of sympathy and stood in awe at the floral shrine to their mother.

At exactly 9.08 a.m. on Saturday, 6th September, six days after her sudden death, the Princess's final journey started from Kensington Palace. An initial wail of "God Bless You", jarred as the cortege made its gentle progress through streets lined by more than a million silent mourners. Some threw flowers as the cortege passed, many wept.

Eight soldiers served as pallbearers in a party from the Prince of Wales Company of the 1st Battalion Welsh Guards.

(left) The coffin holding Diana, Princess of Wales, returns to Britain from Paris, borne by a Royal Air Force guard of honour and draped in the Royal Standard.

(below) Members of the public queue to pay tribute to their princess at her home in London, Kensington Palace.

(right) The area around Kensington Palace became a sea of flowers.

(below) Floral tributes and messages left at the gates of Buckingham Palace in the week after Diana's death.

The Royal Standard draped the Princess's coffin as it made slow, solemn progress on a gun carriage to Westminster Abbey. One of the family wreaths arranged on top of the coffin bore a message addressed simply to "Mummy".

At St James's Palace, the cortege was joined by hundreds of people representing the workers and beneficiaries of the many charities the Princess had supported. They were led bravely by the Princess's two boys, William and Harry, her brother Earl Spencer, Prince Charles and Prince Philip. From there along the Mall, through Horse Guards Road, Horse Guards Parade and Whitehall to Parliament Square and the Broad Sanctuary, they marched, heads bowed behind the gun carriage.

Inside the Abbey, a congregation of 1,900 friends and family drawn from the disparate worlds of State and politics, Household and charities, pop music, film and fashion gathered for a solemn and moving funeral. It combined the traditional and the modern for a unique tribute which addressed the unique grief which had gripped the nation and the world since the news of Diana's death. Her favourite hymn, "I Vow To Thee, My Country", which had also been sung at her wedding symbolised the personal and public nature of the event. Elton John's rendition of "Candle in the Wind", originally a tribute to Marilyn Monroe, now reworked as a homage to the Princess with the opening the words "Goodbye, England's Rose", will stand forever, in the eyes of most of the world, as the musical climax of a ceremony of great passion and eloquence.

The readings, by the Princess's sisters and by the Prime Minister, Tony Blair, spoke of the public Diana. But the address by Earl Spencer will resonate for time to come. He had a harsh message for the press and raised questions about the future lives of the young Princes, speaking of the balance he wished them to strike between attention to royal duty and the need for their souls "to sing openly" as their mother had wished.

Yet, as applause spread gently into the Abbey

from the crowds outside, to engulf the entire congregation, Lord Spencer's potent juxtaposition of his sister's qualities and frailties also struck a chord. He had spoken of the Princess's mischievous sense of humour, her intuition and her compassion, but also of her insecurities and innermost feelings of suffering "that made it possible for her to connect with her constituency of the rejected".

But above all, Lord Spencer said in his closing sentence, he was proud to be able to call his sister "the unique, the complex, the extraordinary and irreplaceable Diana whose beauty, both internal and external, will never be extinguished from our minds".

A minute's silence preceded the departure of the coffin from the Abbey. Along the sunny streets of London, once more lined with alternately silent, then gently applauding crowds, the hearse made its way to the motorway towards Diana's final resting place. She was buried in a private family ceremony in a newly consecrated grave on an island in the grounds of her childhood home, Althorp.

(left) Diana's coffin on the gun carriage as the cortege passes Admiralty Arch on the way to Westminster Abbey.

(below) Five hundred members of the Princess's main charities walked in procession behind her coffin.

The gun carriage carrying Diana's coffin is followed by Prince William and Prince Harry, Earl Spencer, the Prince of Wales and the Duke of Edinburgh in Parliament Square.

(right) Soldiers of the Welsh Guards carry
the coffin into Westminster Abbey.

(below) United in grief, the family arrive
at Westminster Abbey.

(left) The coffin passes the tomb of the unknown soldier, adorned with flowers from Diana's sons and brother.

(below) Thousands of mourners watched the Abbey service on giant screens in Hyde Park.

Thousands of mourners lined the hearse's route from
London to the Spencer family home at Althorp
in Northamptonshire. Many threw flowers in its path.

(overleaf) The grounds of Althorp where Diana is buried
on the island at the centre of the lake.

113

DIANA REMEMBERED

*She was the people's princess
and that is how she will remain in our
hearts and our memories for ever.*

Prime Minister Tony Blair

*Princess Diana will be missed as
a warm, compassionate and caring
person. I was tremendously impressed
by her. She was undoubtedly one of
the best ambassadors of Great Britain.*

Nelson Mandela

*Diana was the very essence of
compassion, of duty, of style, of beauty.
All over the world she was a symbol
of selfless humanity, a standard bearer
for the rights of the truly downtrodden,
a very British girl who transcended
nationality.*

Earl Spencer

It will be a very lucky baby to have Diana as a mother. She adores children and they adore her.

Earl Spencer, Diana's late father

To sanctify your memory would be to miss out on the very core of your being, your wonderfully mischievous sense of humour with a laugh that bent you double.

Earl Spencer

Her beauty was her triumph. It was her badge of survival, her mark of courage and of her ability to accommodate her own sorrows. That, instinctively and perhaps subconsciously, is why people loved her: because she had come through and in the process had grown into someone quite different and much larger than the person she had been before. In some ways some of us have never recognised before, we loved her.

Adam Nicolson in the *Telegraph*

You could not do my work and I could not do yours. We are both working for God. Let us do something beautiful for him.

Mother Teresa

I want to walk into a room, be it a hospice for the dying or a hospital for sick children and feel that I am needed. I want to do, not just to be.

Diana, Princess of Wales

Princess Diana was one of the first and most committed champions of this issue. It will be a struggle for the Aids community to come to terms with her death.

Nick Partridge, The Terence Higgins Trust

If I should die and leave you here awhile,
Be not like others, sore undone who keep
Long vigils by the silent dust, and weep.
For my sake — turn again to life and smile,
Nerving thy heart and trembling hand to do
Something to comfort other hearts than thine
Complete those dear unfinished tasks of mine
And I, perchance, may therein comfort you.

A. Price Hughes
read at Diana's funeral by her sister
Lady Sarah McCorquodale